THE BIRTHDAY BOOK

Illustrated by Jane Ike

A GOLDEN PRESS BOOK

Western Publishing Company, Inc.
New York, New York • Racine, Wisconsin

© 1970 by Western Publishing Company, Inc.
All rights reserved. Produced in U.S.A.

On my birthday I am going to have a party.
And there will be many surprises!

I will invite all my friends.

They will wear their best party clothes.

Mother will bake a surprise birthday cake.
It might be chocolate . . . with pink frosting on top.

And it will have candles.

Balloons and streamers will fill the house:
red ones, yellow, pink, and blue ones!

My friends will be surprised.

We will all wear party hats and blow our party horns.

There will be lots of noise.

Then we will play games—Pin the Tail on the Donkey and Musical Chairs.

There will be prizes for the winners.

Soon it will be time to open the presents.
Every package will be a surprise.

There might be a book in one of the packages.

Or a drum—*rum-tum-tum.*

Or a swing. That would be a surprise!

Or a cat—I'd like that!

Then Mother will light
the candles on the cake.

I will blow them out with one big puff!
All my friends will sing "Happy Birthday."

"Thank you," I will say.
Then I will tell them how old I am.
I might even sing.

We will eat lots of ice cream
and birthday cake.

Next year I will have another birthday party . . .
with surprises.
And there will be one more candle on the cake!